ROCKFORD PUBLIC LIBRARY

3 1112 01617675 8

W9-BJL-402

J 641.5944 WAL
Waldee, Lynne Marie
Cooking the French way :
revised and expanded to
include new low-fat and
vegetarian recipes

040909

WITHDRAWN

ROCKFORD PUBLIC LIBRARY

Rockford, Illinois

www.rockfordpubliclibrary.org

815-965-9511

COOKING
THE
FRENCH
WAY

Copyright © 2002 by Lerner Publications Company

All rights reserved. International copyright secured. No part
of this book may be reproduced, stored in a retrieval system,
or transmitted in any form or by any means—electronic,
mechanical, photocopying, recording, or otherwise—without the prior written permission of Lerner Publications
Company, except for the inclusion of brief quotations in an
acknowledged review.

Lerner Publications Company
A division of Lerner Publishing Group
241 First Avenue North
Minneapolis, MN 55401 U.S.A.

Website address: www.lernerbooks.com

Library of Congress Cataloging-in-Publication Data

Waldee, Lynne Marie.
    Cooking the French way / by Lynne Marie Waldee—Rev. & expanded.
        p.   cm. — (Easy menu ethnic cookbooks)
    Includes index.
    Summary: An introduction to the cooking of France, featuring basic
recipes for everyday breakfast, lunch and dinner dishes, as well as typical
menus and a brief description of the special features of a French table
setting.
        ISBN: 0–8225–4106–8 (lib. bdg. : alk. paper)
        1. Cookery, French. [1. Cookery, French. 2. France—Social life and
customs.] I. Title. II. Series.
TX719.W28 2002
641.5944—dc21   00–012121

Manufactured in the United States of America
1 2 3 4 5 6 – JR – 07 06 05 04 03 02

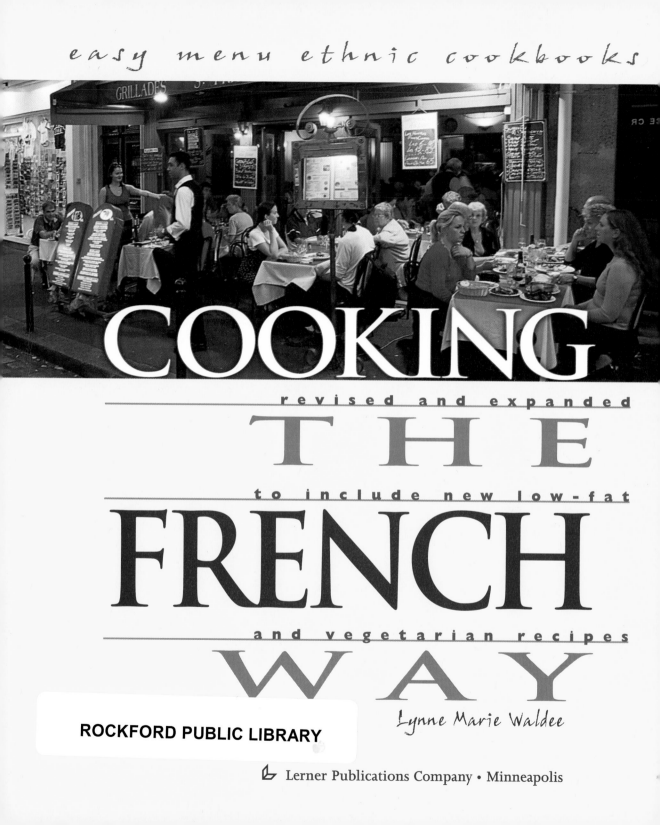

easy menu ethnic cookbooks

COOKING

revised and expanded

THE

to include new low-fat

FRENCH

and vegetarian recipes

WAY

Lynne Marie Waldee

ROCKFORD PUBLIC LIBRARY

Lerner Publications Company • Minneapolis

Contents

Introduction

The people of France consider cooking a fine art. Just as an artist carves out a statue hidden within a block of stone, a French cook brings out the flavor locked inside each simple vegetable and piece of meat. The French cook then arranges the food so that its shapes and colors are combined in the most attractive way possible.

A French saying describes the attitude of French cooks toward their art: *L'excès en tout est défaut*—"excess is always a fault." In other words, you can have too much of a good thing. French cooks use strong flavors, such as garlic, in small amounts so that they will not overpower other flavors. In fact, the most important rule in French cooking is not to use too much of any one ingredient.

Leg of lamb is a traditional French holiday meal. (See recipe on page 60.)

French Cooking

There are two distinctly different kinds of cooking in France. One kind is quite grand and the other is like home cooking. The recipes in this book are of the "home cooking" variety—delicious and easy to fix. But it is interesting to know a little about the grand type of French cooking, too. After all, once you have mastered the dishes in this book, you may want to try something more difficult!

Hundreds of years ago, the chefs who worked for the kings and queens of France developed *haute* or *grande cuisine*. This kind of cooking featured huge, complicated meals that took hours of preparation and often included unusual ingredients such as rare wines and exotic fruits.

When the French nobility was overthrown in the 1789 French Revolution, the chefs who had developed haute cuisine fled to other parts of Europe. The art of this fine cooking, however, was not lost. The French chefs spread its fame throughout Europe and even to the United States. This very special and difficult type of cooking is still practiced in modern times by famous chefs in elegant restaurants.

The other kind of French cooking is called *cuisine bourgeoise*. It is the kind of home cooking you would find in a small restaurant or inn or in the home of a typical French family. Old French home recipes, which have been handed down from generation to generation, are tasty and nourishing.

The Regions of France

Geography has an important effect on the cooking of each region of France. For instance, Normandy, on the northern coast, has many fields where cattle graze and orchards grow. The region's cooking, therefore, features apples, cream, and cheeses. Brittany, a province on the northwest coast, has very poor land, so the region does not have many edible plants or grazing animals. Instead, its riches come from

English
Channel

BELGIUM

LUXEMBOURG

GERMANY

Seine River

NORMANDY

Marne River

★ Paris

LORRAINE

BRITTANY

Rhine River

Loire River

**Atlantic
Ocean**

SWITZERLAND

*Bay of
Biscay*

FRANCE

• Lyons

Rhône River

• Bordeaux

ITALY

Garrone River

• Bayonne

BASQUE
AREA

PROVENCE

Nice •

• Toulouse

Marseilles •

SPAIN

CORSICA

Mediterranean Sea

the ocean. Cooks in Brittany prepare fine soups and other dishes using all sorts of seafood, including lobsters, shrimp, mussels, and saltwater fish.

In some regions of France, cooking is strongly affected by the traditions of neighboring countries. In the south of France, the snow-covered Pyrénées Mountains are near Spain. The cooking of that region resembles Spanish cooking. It uses tomatoes, peppers, and sausages. In southeastern France, the province of Provence borders

Italy. Olives, as well as many herbs, grow on Provence's gently rolling hills. In the cooking of Provence, you will find plenty of olive oil and herbs such as basil, thyme, and rosemary—ingredients also used in the cooking of northern Italy.

Dining in France

If French cooking can be called an art, then dining in France can be called a ceremony! The eating of a well-prepared meal is considered one of the important pleasures of daily life. Many dining customs that have grown through centuries are still part of the daily routine in France. At mealtime, family members gather around the table. They talk while they eat, sharing ideas and telling stories of their day's experiences. After the meal, family members go back to their own routines, but each is left with a feeling of well-being that comes from enjoying a good meal and pleasant conversation.

Mealtime in France is a time for friends and family to enjoy food and conversation.

The recipes in this book will show you the many pleasures of French home cooking. You can enjoy preparing and eating these meals yourself, but you may enjoy them even more if you eat them French-style—in a leisurely way with your family.

Holidays and Festivals

Joie de vivre, which means "joy of living," is a commonly used expression throughout France. The phrase sums up the French approach to life—that it's to be enjoyed. What better way to celebrate life than through festivals, holiday gatherings, and good food?

Three out of every four French people belong to the Roman Catholic Church. Although a good number of the French are not practicing Catholics, many of the festivities in which they take part throughout the year honor religious holidays. Easter is the most important holiday.

Easter, or les Pâques, observances begin in early spring on Good Friday. On this day, church bells in villages and towns throughout France stop ringing. Since the bells usually announce the beginning of Mass (church services) and mark every new hour of the day, the silence is unusual. It serves to remind French Catholics of the solemn time between Jesus' death and resurrection. When children ask why the bells don't ring, parents tell them the story they were told as children. According to French folklore, the bells fly away to Rome, Italy, carrying the sorrow of those who believe that Jesus died on Good Friday. On the morning of Easter Sunday, when Jesus is believed to have risen from the dead, the bells return. Along the way, the bells drop eggs and chocolates in the yards of the faithful. On Sunday, the bells ring once again to announce the beginning of Easter Mass.

After Mass festivities continue at the family home with a four- or five-course meal, followed by dessert. Favorite Easter foods include foie gras—a goose-liver pâté—lamb, salmon, asparagus, new potatoes, and strawberries. Coffee, liqueur, and chocolates round out the meal.

For weeks before the Easter holiday, French bakeries churn out chocolates shaped like chickens, rabbits, fish, or bells. Some of the candies are quite elaborate. Most of the fish have scales, and some are stuffed with lots of tiny candy fish. A ribbon secures the big fish's middle. When someone pulls open the bow, the tiny fish spill from the opening.

Noël, or Christmas, is a time for families to celebrate together. On Christmas Eve, French children place their shoes, called *sabots*, in front of the fireplace. They hope for a visit from le Père Noël—Father Christmas, or Santa Claus—who will fill the shoes with presents, (and not a spanking from le Père Fouettard, the one who punishes the children who've been bad!).

At midnight French families attend Christmas Eve Mass, where they sing hymns and light candles to honor the newborn Christ child. After Mass it is the French tradition to enjoy a meal called *le réveillon*, which means "to wake up to a new day." Restaurants stay open all night serving the feast, which may consist of oysters, sausages, wine, baked ham, roast chicken, salads, fruit, and pastries. Different regions have different specialties, but Christ cakes, which are decorated with sugar and shaped like the baby Jesus, are popular all over the country. *Pain calendeau*, or Christmas loaf, is the dessert of choice in southern France. The server cuts the loaf crosswise and gives one half to a poor person before cutting up the other half. In Paris, celebrants enjoy *bûche de Noël*, a cake shaped like a Yule log, for dessert. The main course can vary, too. A roasted goose is the main course of le réveillon in the Alsace region in northeastern France. Turkey and chestnuts are preferred in the Burgundy region of eastern France. In Provence le réveillon is called *le gros souper* (the big supper). It is a tradition in Provence to end the meal with thirteen desserts, symbolizing Christ and the twelve apostles. The host serves all of the desserts at once and the guests are expected to sample them all. Desserts include dried fruit, *pompe à l'huile* (pastry with olive oil), fudge, candied fruit, marzipan, cookies, and the Yule log.

After dinner, the French head for home. Before going to bed, they may light a candle in honor of the Virgin Mary. They let it burn through the night. French kids wake up early on Christmas morning to see what le Père Noël left them.

French children also look forward to Epiphany, celebrated on January 6. The holiday honors the first time Jesus appeared before the Three Kings. This is the day that French children are showered with gifts. The French celebrate the day with a special cake called *galette des rois*—a round puff pastry filled with almond cream. A bean, called a *fève*, is baked inside the cake. The *fève* represents the Christ child. Whoever finds the bean has the honor of wearing a cardboard crown for the day. Although Epiphany is a religious holiday, French people of all backgrounds take part in the festivities.

All French celebrate Bastille Day, too. On July 14, the French have a party to honor the end of the rule of the French monarchy and the beginning of the first French Republic. On this day in the year 1789,

Street performers entertain the crowd in St. Jeannet, France.

Dancers in traditional dress perform at a French harvest festival in Nice.

French people attacked the Bastille prison in Paris. To them, the prison was a symbol of the absolute power of the monarchy. This event triggered the French Revolution.

These days Bastille Day represents liberty and democracy for the French people. They celebrate with a big military parade down the Champs-Elysées, a well-known boulevard in Paris. People gather at bistros and cafés for good food, music, and dance. After the sun sets, fireworks brighten the skies all over the country.

Other prominent national holidays include May Day on May 1, when the French give *muguets*, or lilies of the valley, to friends and neighbors. The flower is believed to bring good luck. All Saints' Day, which falls on November 1, is a day to remember relatives and friends who have died. The French ring in the New Year with parties, champagne, and food.

When there's not a religious or national holiday to celebrate, the French still have regional festivals to look forward to. Most of these parties honor a local saint or a big harvest. In the Provence region, the French celebrate many harvests. In June the people of Gorbio give thanks for the olive harvest with the *procession dai limaca*. In Sault the French ring in the lavender crops in August with the Fête de la Lavande. September is when people in Arles, France, celebrate the Camargue rice harvest. In the same month, those living in Peyruis honor the apple harvest, while people all over France enjoy grape harvest festivities. The fruits of these harvests take center stage in the food prepared for the festivals.

The way that the French choose to celebrate reflects their love of the good things in life. In the regions throughout France, cooks turn to the ingredients they have on hand to make the best foods for the occasion.

ABRICOT MARRON 15F
CHANTILLY CHOCOLAT 20F
SUCRE 12F

Before You Begin

Cooking any dish, plain or fancy, is easier and more fun if you are familiar with its ingredients. French cooking makes use of some ingredients that you may not know. Sometimes special cookware is used, too, although the recipes in this book can easily be prepared with ordinary utensils and pans.

Before you start cooking, read "The Careful Cook" on the following page and study the "dictionary" of terms and special ingredients. Read through the recipe you want to try from beginning to end. Then you will be ready to shop for ingredients and to organize the cookware you will need. Once you have assembled everything, you can begin to cook.

Crepes are a common French food and cooking them is an art form.

The Careful Cook

Whenever you cook, there are certain safety rules you must always keep in mind. Even experienced cooks follow these rules when they are in the kitchen.

- Always wash your hands before handling food. Thoroughly wash all raw vegetables and fruits to remove dirt, chemicals, and insecticides. Wash uncooked poultry, fish, and meat under cold water.
- Use a cutting board when cutting up vegetables and fruits. Don't cut them up in your hand! And be sure to cut in a direction *away* from you and your fingers.
- Long hair or loose clothing can easily catch fire if brought near the burners of a stove. If you have long hair, tie it back before you start cooking.
- Turn all pot handles toward the back of the stove so that you will not catch your sleeves or jewelry on them. This is especially important when younger brothers and sisters are around. They could easily knock off a pot and get burned.
- Always use a pot holder to steady hot pots or to take pans out of the oven. Don't use a wet cloth on a hot pan because the steam it produces could burn you.
- Lift the lid of a steaming pot with the opening away from you so that you will not get burned.
- If you get burned, hold the burn under cold running water. Do not put grease or butter on it. Cold water helps to take the heat out, but grease or butter will only keep it in.
- If grease or cooking oil catches fire, throw baking soda or salt at the bottom of the flame to put it out. (Water will *not* put out a grease fire.) Call for help, and try to turn all the stove burners to "off."

Cooking Utensils

crepe pan—There are many pans available that are designed specifically for crepe-making, but almost any low-sided pan with a cooking surface 6 to 8 inches in diameter will work just as well.

jelly-roll pan—A flat, thin cooking sheet, 1 inch deep, usually about 11 by 14 inches

pastry blender—A U-shaped wire utensil with a handle, used to combine butter or shortening with flour when making dough. If you do not have a pastry blender, use a fork or a food processor.

whisk—A wire utensil used for beating food by hand

Cooking Terms

boil—To heat a liquid over high heat until bubbles form and rise rapidly to the surface

brown—To cook food quickly in fat over high heat so that the surface turns an even brown

grate—To cut into tiny pieces by rubbing the food against a grater; to shred

hard-cook—To boil an egg in its shell until both the yolk and white are firm

mince—To chop food into very small pieces

preheat—To allow an oven to warm up to a certain temperature before putting food in it

sauté—To fry quickly over high heat in oil or fat, stirring or turning the food to prevent burning

shred—To tear or cut into small pieces, either by hand or with a grater

simmer—To cook over low heat in liquid kept just below its boiling point. Bubbles may occasionally rise to the surface.

Special Ingredients

almond paste— A sweet, thick paste that is made from ground almonds and is used to fill pastries and cakes

bay leaf—The dried leaf of the bay (also called laurel) tree. It is used to season meats, poultry, soups, and stews.

chives—A member of the onion family whose thin, green stalks are chopped and used to garnish salads as well as fish, egg, cheese, potato, and other vegetable dishes

Dijon-style mustard—A commercially prepared condiment (an ingredient used to enhance the flavor of food) made from mustard seed, white wine, vinegar, salt, and spices

garlic—An herb whose distinctively flavored bulb is used in many dishes. Fresh garlic can usually be found in the produce department of a supermarket. Each bulb can be broken up into several small sections called cloves. Most recipes use only one or two finely chopped cloves of this very strong herb. Before you chop up a clove of garlic, you will have to remove the brittle, papery covering that surrounds it.

Gruyère cheese—A hard, tangy, light yellow cheese from the Gruyère district of Switzerland

leek—An herb in the onion family, but milder in taste than an onion. The bulb of the leek is used to flavor soups and stews and is also served as a vegetable.

nutmeg—A fragrant spice that is ground and most often used in desserts

olive oil—An oil made from pressed olives and used in cooking and for dressing salads

Parmesan cheese—A very hard, sharply flavored, yellowish Italian cheese that is usually grated for use in cooking and is also used as a garnish for soups and salads

puff pastry—Sheets of thin, flaky pastry that you can purchase frozen at any grocery store red wine vinegar—A vinegar made with red wine that is often mixed with oil for dressing salads

safflower oil—A light, vegetable oil pressed from the seeds of the safflower herb

thyme—The leaves of a bushy shrub that grows mainly in California and France. It is used as an herb in cooking and has a very strong flavor.

Healthy and Low-Fat Cooking Tips

Nutritionists use the words "French paradox" to describe the French diet. Why? Because all of the butter and heavy cream in French foods can lead to high cholesterol and high blood pressure. Despite this, the French are less likely to die of heart disease than Americans. Recent studies point to some reasons why the French diet keeps heart disease in check.

The French eat almost twice as many fruits and vegetables as Americans. And since the French shop daily for fresh fruits and vegetables, they are likely to pick out whatever looks good each day. So they eat a wider variety of fruits and vegetables. The French also use a lot of olive oil in their cooking. Not only does olive oil have a much lower cholesterol content than butter, the fat that the oil contains is easier for the body to digest than the fat found in butter. Studies have also shown that the time French families devote to meals makes a difference. The French take one, sometimes two, hours for lunch and dinner. It is a time to visit with family and friends, relax, and enjoy the food. As a result, the French enjoy lower levels of stress than Americans, who are more likely to eat in a hurry.

As a cook, there are many things you can do to prepare healthy, low-fat meals. Here are a few general tips for adapting the recipes in this book. Throughout the book, you'll also find specific suggestions for individual recipes—and don't worry, they'll still taste delicious!

Many recipes call for butter or oil to sauté vegetables or other ingredients. Using olive oil or canola oil instead of butter lowers the amount of saturated fat right away, but you can also reduce the amount of oil you use—often by half. Sprinkling a little salt on the vegetables brings out their natural juices, so less oil is needed. It's also a good idea to use a small, nonstick frying pan if you decide to use less oil than the recipe calls for. You may also use nonstick cooking sprays to grease cooking dishes.

Another common substitution for butter is margarine. Before making this substitution, consider the recipe. Many French desserts call for butter. It's often best to use butter. Margarine may noticeably change the taste or consistency of the food.

When a recipe calls for sour cream, cut the fat content by using a low-fat variety or plain, nonfat yogurt as substitutes. Drain the yogurt through a paper filter before using.

Cheese is a common source of unwanted fat. Many cheeses are available in reduced or nonfat varieties, but keep in mind that these varieties often don't melt as well. Another easy way to reduce the amount of fat from cheese is simply to use less of it! To avoid losing flavor, you might try using a stronger tasting cheese. For some recipes, you might like to substitute half and half or evaporated skim milk for heavy whipping cream to lower the fat content. This substitution works well in recipes for soups and quiche. But in recipes for sauces, it's best to use whipping cream, as the sauce's texture relies on it. Not using a sauce is also an option.

Lower the fat content of quiche and other egg dishes by using an egg substitute in place of real eggs. When broth is called for, use low-fat and nonfat canned varieties to cut the fat.

There are many ways to prepare meals that are good for you and still taste great. As you become a more experienced cook, try experimenting with recipes and substitutions to find the methods that work best for you.

METRIC CONVERSIONS

Cooks in the United States measure both liquid and solid ingredients using standard containers based on the 8-ounce cup and the tablespoon. These measurements are based on volume, while the metric system of measurement is based on both weight (for solids) and volume (for liquids). To convert from U.S. fluid tablespoons, ounces, quarts, and so forth to metric liters is a straightforward conversion, using the chart below. However, since solids have different weights—one cup of rice does not weigh the same as one cup of grated cheese, for example—many cooks who use the metric system have kitchen scales to weigh different ingredients. The chart below will give you a good starting point for basic conversions to the metric system.

MASS (weight)

1 ounce (oz.)	=	28.0 grams (g)
8 ounces	=	227.0 grams
1 pound (lb.) or 16 ounces	=	0.45 kilograms (kg)
2.2 pounds	=	1.0 kilogram

LIQUID VOLUME

1 teaspoon (tsp.)	=	5.0 milliliters (ml)
1 tablespoon (tbsp.)	=	15.0 milliliters
1 fluid ounce (oz.)	=	30.0 milliliters
1 cup (c.)	=	240 milliliters
1 pint (pt.)	=	480 milliliters
1 quart (qt.)	=	0.95 liters (l)
1 gallon (gal.)	=	3.80 liters

LENGTH

¼ inch (in.)	=	0.6 centimeters (cm)
½ inch	=	1.25 centimeters
1 inch	=	2.5 centimeters

TEMPERATURE

212°F	=	100°C (boiling point of water)
225°F	=	110°C
250°F	=	120°C
275°F	=	135°C
300°F	=	150°C
325°F	=	160°C
350°F	=	180°C
375°F	=	190°C
400°F	=	200°C

(To convert temperature in Fahrenheit to Celsius, subtract 32 and multiply by .56)

PAN SIZES

8-inch cake pan	=	20 x 4-centimeter cake pan
9-inch cake pan	=	23 x 3.5-centimeter cake pan
11 x 7-inch baking pan	=	28 x 18-centimeter baking pan
13 x 9-inch baking pan	=	32.5 x 23-centimeter baking pan
9 x 5-inch loaf pan	=	23 x 13-centimeter loaf pan
2-quart casserole	=	2-liter casserole

A French Table

Simplicity is the key to decorating the table in most French homes. Because the appearance, smell, and taste of carefully prepared foods are the central concerns of the French cook, decorations and extra dishes on the table are kept to a minimum. Simple place settings and cloth napkins (never paper) are used on plain or checked cloths.

Fragrant flowers are never used on the table because their scent could detract from the aroma of the food and, therefore, the enjoyment of the meal. But a small collection of condiments is usually found on the table. These often include oil and vinegar in cruets (glass bottles), wine-based French mustard in a bowl with a small wooden spoon, salt, and peppercorns in a pepper mill. Such seasonings add sparkle to the meal, and their containers decorate the table.

Family mealtimes offer a time to enjoy the taste of good food as well as to share in one another's company.

A French Menu

Although the French usually eat a big, leisurely lunch and dinner, breakfast is small. A cup of coffee or hot chocolate and a pastry or bread is typical fare. Below are two dinner menus with shopping lists of the items you'll need to prepare the meals. All the recipes can be found in this book.

DINNER #1

Green salad with vinaigrette dressing

Quiche Lorraine

Fresh asparagus with aioli

Crepes with strawberries

SHOPPING LIST:

Produce

1 medium tomato (for vegetarian quiche only)
1 small head Boston lettuce
1 small head romaine or 1 medium head iceberg lettuce
1 bunch fresh parsley
garlic
2 pt. fresh strawberries
1 lb. fresh asparagus
1 lemon

Dairy/Egg/Meat

1 dozen eggs
1 c. whipping cream
milk
butter
4 to 6 oz. Swiss cheese
cottage cheese
sour cream
8 oz. bacon (for meat-based quiche)

Miscellaneous

olive oil
safflower oil
salt
pepper
flour
sugar
red wine vinegar

DINNER #2

Potato-and-leek soup

Sautéed chicken

Glazed carrots

Green salad with
vinaigrette dressing

Chocolate mousse

SHOPPING LIST:

Produce

1 small head Boston
   lettuce
1 small head romaine or
   1 medium-sized head
   iceberg lettuce
1 bunch fresh parsley
garlic
3 oz. fresh, sliced
   mushrooms
1 lb. carrots
3 medium potatoes
3 medium leeks
1 bunch fresh chives

Dairy/Egg/Meat

1 2½- to 3-lb. chicken,
   cut into serving pieces
butter or margarine
6 eggs
milk
1 pt. heavy cream, half and
   half, or evaporated skim
   milk

Canned/Bottled/Boxed

1½ c. canned chicken broth
2 unsweetened chocolate
   baking squares
1 semisweet chocolate
   baking square
1 envelope unsweetened
   gelatin

Miscellaneous

salt
pepper
flour
thyme
red wine vinegar
olive oil
bay leaves
sugar
vanilla extract

Lunch/Le Déjeuner

In the countryside and small towns of France, the main meal is served around noon. A smaller meal is usually served in the evening, between 7 and 8 P.M. People who live in the large cities of France often have their small meal in the middle of the day, as most North Americans do. The recipes given here will make a delicious noon lunch, or you can eat them for a light evening meal.

Hearty soups are often served as the main course of a French luncheon. The soup is always accompanied by crusty French bread, which may be used to soak up the last drops of broth. The practice of mopping up a soup or sauce with bread is not considered bad manners in France. In fact, it is done at almost every meal at which a delicious soup or sauce is served.

Eggs are rarely served for breakfast in France but are often used in luncheon or dinner dishes such as omelets, soufflés, and quiches. Salads are usually served between the main course and dessert. A light dessert of cheese and fruit completes a typical French luncheon. A tasty combination is Brie cheese and crisp, tart apples.

This delicious ham and broccoli crepe with Mornay sauce can be made with onions and mushrooms for a vegetarian option. (See recipe on page 38.)

Potato-and-Leek Soup/*Potage Parmentier*

This creamy soup, along with French bread, makes a delicious and filling meal. Leftover soup keeps well in the refrigerator and can be reheated the next day. (Make sure that you don't boil the soup because boiling will make the dairy curdle, or form lumps.) This soup can also be eaten cold. The French call the cold version vichyssoise.

3 medium-sized potatoes, peeled and sliced ⅛-inch thick

3 medium-sized leeks, washed thoroughly and sliced ⅛-inch thick (do not use the tough, dark green part), or 3 medium-sized yellow onions, thinly sliced

3 10¾-oz. cans (about 4½ c.) chicken broth

1 chicken-broth can of cold water

½ c. whipping cream (add up to an extra ½ c. milk if you like your soup thin), or half and half, or evaporated skim milk

2 tbsp. butter or margarine (optional)

2 tsp. salt

¼ tsp. pepper

chopped chives

1. Combine potatoes, leeks or onions, chicken broth*, and water in a large heavy pot or saucepan and cover.

2. Bring to a boil over medium-high heat. Reduce heat and simmer 35 to 45 minutes or until vegetables are tender.

3. Without draining off broth, mash vegetables in the pan with a vegetable (potato) masher until they are fairly smooth. (If they will not mash easily, soup has not cooked long enough. Let it simmer 10 to 15 minutes longer.)

4. Add cream (or half and half, or evaporated skim milk), butter (optional), salt, and pepper. Heat soup just to the boiling point. (Do not boil.)

5. Sprinkle each serving with chives.

Preparation time: 1 hour 15 minutes
Serves 4 to 5

*To lower the fat content of this soup, use low-fat chicken broth and substitute evaporated skim milk for the whipping cream. To turn this into a vegetarian dish, substitute vegetable broth for chicken broth.

Quiche Lorraine

Quiche Lorraine, a main-dish pie, is traditionally made of cream, eggs, and bacon. Many cooks add cheese to these ingredients. This specialty takes its name from the area in northeastern France called Lorraine, which is famous for its bacon.

4 eggs

1 c. whipping cream

¼ tsp. salt

dash of pepper

¼ tsp. nutmeg

1 9-inch deep-dish unbaked pie shell (shell can be bought frozen in a store)

4 to 6 oz. Swiss cheese, thinly sliced or grated (1 to 1½ c. when grated)

8 oz. bacon*, lightly browned and crumbled

1. Preheat the oven to 350°F.

2. In a medium-sized mixing bowl, beat eggs, cream, salt, pepper, and nutmeg with an eggbeater or a whisk.

3. With a fork, prick sides and bottom of unbaked pie shell about every half inch. (This will keep pie shell from shrinking or bubbling while it is baking.)

4. Make 2 or 3 layers of alternating cheese and bacon bits in bottom of pie shell. Pour egg-and-cream mixture over this.

5. Bake 45 to 50 minutes, or until quiche is golden brown and puffy.

6. Let cool a few minutes and slice into serving pieces. Refrigerate leftovers and reheat or eat cold the next day.

Preparation and cooking time: 1 hour 30 minutes
Serves 4 to 5

To lower the fat content of this dish, cut the amount of bacon in half. Also look for lean varieties or use turkey bacon. To make this a vegetarian dish, substitute 1 fresh tomato, chopped, for the bacon.

Nicoise Salad/ Salade Niçoise

This vegetable salad is a hearty main meal by itself. If you want to serve it as one course of a larger meal, leave out the tuna fish. You can also vary the other ingredients in this recipe. Try adding carrots, celery, peas, slices of hard-cooked eggs, or slivered almonds. Experiment and enjoy!

1 small head of lettuce

6 medium-sized cold cooked potatoes, or 1-lb. can small whole white potatoes

½ lb. fresh green beans or 1 10-oz. package frozen green beans, cooked, chilled, and cut into ½-inch lengths

6 tomatoes, quartered

½ c. vinaigrette dressing (see page 36)

1 13-oz. can tuna, drained* (optional)

black or green olives for garnish (optional)

1. Wash and separate lettuce leaves, throwing away any that are wilted or discolored. Pat lettuce leaves dry. Arrange leaves decoratively in a large, shallow serving plate and set aside.

2. In a large mixing bowl, combine potatoes, beans, and tomatoes. Pour vinaigrette dressing over vegetables. Using 2 spoons, carefully toss vegetables until they are thoroughly coated.

3. Spoon vegetables onto lettuce leaves and top with mound of tuna and/or olives. (Or if you prefer, arrange the vegetables and tuna as shown in the photo.)

4. Serve immediately.

Preparation time: 30 minutes
Serves 4 to 5

*For a healthier salad, use water-packed tuna instead of oil-packed.

Fish is often used to accentuate the nicoise salad. Try it with tuna or even anchovies if you're feeling adventuresome.

Green Salad / Salade Verte

Green salads are served after the main dish "to clear the palate." This means that the lettuce and light dressing refresh your taste buds, preparing them for the new flavors of the dessert to follow.

Salad:

1 small head of Boston lettuce

1 small head of romaine or
    1 medium-sized head of iceberg
    lettuce

3 tbsp. chopped fresh parsley

Vinaigrette:

1 clove garlic

1 tsp. salt (optional)

3 tbsp. red wine vinegar

¼ tsp. pepper

6 tbsp. olive or vegetable oil

1. To prepare salad greens, wash Boston lettuce and romaine thoroughly. Drain by placing leaves on paper towels. Place clean greens in a plastic bag along with the paper towels, to absorb any remaining water. Refrigerate for at least half an hour.

2. Tear greens into small pieces and place them in a large salad bowl. Sprinkle with parsley.

3. Chop garlic into very fine pieces and put in a small bowl.

4. Use the back of a spoon to mash garlic. Then mix it with salt.

5. Add vinegar and pepper, stirring until smooth.

6. Place in a small jar with a tight-fitting lid. Add oil, screw on lid, and shake until well blended.

7. Pour about half of the vinaigrette dressing over greens. Toss with a fork and spoon until greens are well coated and no dressing remains in bottom of bowl.

Preparation time: 10 to 15 minutes
Enough for 4 to 5 salad servings

Basic Crepe Batter

These delicate pancakes made of egg-and-flour batter are both fun to make and delicious. They are often filled with meat, fish, or vegetables, covered with a sauce, and served as a main course. Dessert crepes are made with a sweeter batter and are often filled with fruit (see page 52).

4 eggs

¼ tsp. salt

2 c. all-purpose flour

2¼ c. milk

¼ c. melted butter

1. Combine eggs and salt in a bowl.

2. Alternately stir in flour and milk. Then beat with a whisk or electric mixer until creamy.

3. Beat in melted butter.

4. Chill batter at least 1 hour.

5. Heat a crepe pan on medium-high heat. Pour the crepe batter into the pan as you would to make a pancake. Swirl the batter to coat the entire bottom of the pan.

6. Cook for about 2 minutes or until the bottom of the crepe becomes firm.

7. Use a fork to gently lift the crepe from the pan. Quickly flip the crepe to cook the other side.

8. Cook for 1 minute or until the crepe just starts to brown. Move the crepe to a plate.

Preparation time: 2 hours
Makes 32 to 36 crepes

Ham and Broccoli Crepes with Mornay Sauce/
Crêpes au Broccoli et Jambon avec Sauce Mornay

Crepes:

1 lb. fresh broccoli spears or 2 8-oz. packages frozen broccoli spears

12 basic crepes (see page 37)

12 thin slices deli ham* (or ¼ c. chopped onions and 2 c. chopped, fresh mushrooms)

Mornay sauce (see page 39)

1. Fill a large saucepan with water and bring to a boil. Add broccoli and boil for 1 to 2 minutes. Drain and slice each spear in half.

2. If you are making the vegetarian version, heat 1 tbsp. of olive oil in a skillet over medium-high heat. Sauté the onions for about 5 minutes, or until translucent. Add the mushrooms and cook until soft. Remove the pan from heat.

3. Preheat the oven to 400°F.

4. Spread out crepes and cover each crepe with a slice of ham or mushroom mix.

5. Place 2 or 3 broccoli spears on top of ham or mushrooms and onions and roll up crepes.

6. Place crepes in a buttered ovenproof dish. Cover with foil and bake for 15 minutes.

7. Cover with Mornay sauce and serve.

Preparation time: 30 minutes
Makes 12 crepes

Mornay Sauce:

1 tbsp. butter

1 tbsp. all-purpose flour

1 c. milk

3 tbsp. grated Swiss cheese

1 tbsp. grated Parmesan cheese

½ tsp. mild prepared mustard
   (Dijon-style is best)

salt and pepper

1. Melt butter in a saucepan.

2. Remove from heat and stir in flour with a whisk.

3. Return to medium heat. Add milk slowly, stirring constantly until sauce is thickened.

4. Add remaining ingredients, salt and pepper to taste, and serve.

Preparation time: 15 minutes
Makes about 1¼ c.

*Try substituting a flavored tofu for the ham.
Many grocery stores and coop markets offer a range of
tasty tofu, such as Thai and Italian. Cut up the tofu
in bite-sized chunks and add to the crepes, following
the directions in Step 4 of the crepe recipe. (You may
prefer to skip the Mornay Sauce if you
choose to add tofu to your crepes.)*

Snack / Le Casse-Croûte

A traditional French custom is to have a mid-afternoon snack of very strong coffee and a pastry or bread. *Brioches* are yeast breads rich in eggs and butter. They make delicious snacks and are generally eaten warm with unsalted butter and jam.

Since brioches are time consuming to prepare at home, many French families buy these treats when they buy their day's supply of bread from one of the many excellent bakeries that can be found all over France. Brioches are also available in American bakeries that sell French breads and pastries.

The recipe on page 42 will make a snack that is something like the French brioche. If you are not able to shop at a French bakery, you can bake this very special treat.

Whether it's chocolate pastry or croque monsieur, *the afternoon snack is customarily flavorful and is served with coffee. (See recipes on pages 42 and 43.)*

Chocolate Pastry / *Brioche au Chocolat*

1 package refrigerated crescent rolls

6 tbsp. semisweet chocolate chips

powdered sugar (enough to sprinkle lightly on each pastry)

1. Preheat the oven to 400°F.

2. Remove the dough according to directions on package. Smooth out perforations (dotted lines) in dough with your fingers and cut dough into 6 rectangles.

3. In the center of each rectangle, place 1 tbsp. of chocolate chips. Bring each of the 4 corners of the rectangle to the middle and seal to make an envelope.

4. Place pastries on an ungreased cookie sheet and bake 10 to 15 minutes or until golden.

5. Remove and place pastries on a cooling rack. Sprinkle tops lightly with powdered sugar.

6. Serve while pastries are slightly warm.

Preparation time: 30 minutes
Makes 6

Croque Monsieur

2 thick slices cooked ham

4 thick slices white bread, with crusts cut off

4 oz. Swiss or Gruyère cheese, grated (1 c. when grated)

3 tbsp. butter*

2 tsp. all-purpose flour

1 c. milk, heated

pepper

1 egg

*To cut the saturated fat content, fry the sandwiches in 1 tbsp. of margarine or olive oil instead of butter. Spraying a nonstick pan with cooking spray is also an option. The sauce can be omitted, too.

1. Put ham slice on each of 2 bread slices. Then press all but 2 tbsp. grated cheese on top of ham.

2. Make sandwiches by firmly pressing another bread slice on top of each.

3. In a saucepan, heat 1 tbsp. butter, stir in flour, and let cook 1 minute.

4. Add warm milk and stir until thick and creamy.

5. Add 2 remaining tbsp. grated cheese. Add pepper to taste. Keep this sauce warm, but do not boil.

6. Beat egg and dip 2 sandwiches in it, making sure both sides of each sandwich are soaked.

7. Melt 2 remaining tbsp. butter in a frying pan. Fry sandwiches until golden and crisp on both sides.

8. Pour cheese sauce over each sandwich and serve.

Preparation time: 30 minutes
Serves 2

Dinner and Dessert/
Le Dîner et le Dessert

The main meal of the day can be quite an event in France. If guests dine with the family, there may be four or five courses, each brought to the table separately, and special wines are chosen to go with the foods being served.

Fancy dinners with many courses may last for several hours. When the dishes are finally cleared away, the diners top off their evening of tasty food and lively conversation with cups of strong black coffee.

At quiet dinners when the family dines alone, plain but delicious home cooking is in order. There are fewer courses, and only ordinary table wine is served. But the tradition of good food and talk is still carried on, for dinner is the one time during the day when the members of the family can be together.

These pork chops Normandy style are a rich, delicious dish that may be served as a main dish at a family meal. (See recipe on page 48.)

Sautéed Chicken / Sauté de Poulet

1 2½- to 3-lb. chicken, cut into
serving pieces

⅓ c. all-purpose flour combined
with ½ tsp. salt,
¼ tsp. thyme, and
¼ tsp. pepper

2 tbsp. butter or margarine

1 tbsp. olive or vegetable oil

½ tsp. thyme

1 bay leaf, finely crumbled

2 cloves garlic, finely chopped

1½ c. canned chicken broth

1 c. fresh mushrooms, sliced

1. Wash chicken pieces under cool
running water. Pat dry with paper
towels.

2. Put seasoned flour in a small, plastic
bag. Place chicken pieces in the bag,
one at a time, and shake to coat
with flour.

3. Heat butter and oil in a large skillet
or heavy pot. Add chicken and
brown on both sides over medium-
high heat. Reduce heat to low and
cook, covered, for 20 minutes,
turning chicken twice.

4. Sprinkle chicken pieces with thyme,
bay leaf, and garlic. Slowly add
chicken broth and mushrooms into
the skillet.

5. Stir gently. Cover the skillet, but
leave a small opening through
which steam can escape. Cook over
low heat for about 30 minutes, or
until about half of the sauce has
cooked away and chicken is tender.

6. Spoon sauce over chicken pieces
when you serve them.

Preparation time: 1 hour
Serves 4

Accented with thyme, bay leaf, and garlic, this sautéed chicken is a savory main course.

Pork Chops Normandy Style/
Côtelettes de Porc Normande

2 tbsp. butter or margarine

1 tbsp. olive or vegetable oil

4 pork chops, about 1 inch thick

1 clove garlic, minced

1 medium-sized onion, thinly sliced

1¼ c. apple cider

¼ tsp. nutmeg

1½ tsp. salt

dash of pepper

1 large tart apple, peeled, cored, and cut into ¼-inch-thick slices

2 tbsp. brown sugar

3 tbsp. whipping cream

Fat-conscious cooks can make this dish without the sauce. The pork chops are quite tasty when made with just apples.

1. Heat butter and oil in a large skillet. Add chops and brown over medium-high heat. Reduce heat slightly and cook chops 6 minutes on each side.

2. Remove chops from the skillet and place on a serving platter. Pour off all but 3 tbsp. fat from the skillet.

3. Put garlic and onion in the skillet and sauté until onions are tender but not browned (about 5 minutes).

4. Add apple cider. Simmer sauce, covered, for 5 minutes.

5. Return pork chops to the skillet. Sprinkle with nutmeg, salt, and pepper. Arrange apple slices over pork chops and sprinkle chops and apples with brown sugar.

6. Cover and simmer for 15 to 20 minutes, or until chops and apples are tender.

7. Stir cream into the skillet with a whisk. Simmer 5 minutes, uncovered.*

8. Spoon apple slices and sauce over pork chops when you serve them.

Preparation time: 1 hour 15 minutes
Serves 4

Potato Cake/ Galette de Pommes de Terre

This buttery potato cake is a delicious side dish that goes well with any kind of meat or fish.

6 medium-sized baking potatoes,
   peeled and thinly sliced

salt and pepper to taste

⅓ c. melted butter or margarine

1. Place a layer of potato slices in the bottom of a greased 9-inch pie plate.

2. Season with small amount of salt and pepper. Repeat until all potato slices have been used.

3. Pour butter evenly over potatoes.

4. Do not cover dish. Cook in a 400°F oven until potatoes are tender (about 50 minutes).

5. Gently loosen the sides and bottom of cake with a spatula. Flip over onto a serving plate. Cut into wedges to serve.

Preparation time: 1 hour 15 minutes
Serves 6

Peas French Style / *Petits Pois à la Française*

2 lb. fresh peas or 1 10-oz. package
    frozen tiny green peas

1 tsp. sugar

½ tsp. salt

dash of pepper

2 tbsp. minced fresh parsley

1½ c. finely shredded lettuce

¼ c. butter or margarine

1 tbsp. water

1. If you have fresh peas, shell just before using.

2. Place all ingredients in a medium-sized saucepan and stir gently.

3. Cover tightly and cook over low heat for 20 minutes or until peas are tender. (For frozen peas, cover tightly and cook over low heat for 8 minutes. Then stir with a fork to break up any remaining frozen peas. Replace cover and cook 3 to 7 minutes longer or until peas are tender.)

Preparation time: 45 minutes
Serves 4

Glazed Carrots / *Carottes Vichy*

1 lb. carrots, peeled and thinly sliced

¼ c. water

dash of salt

3 tbsp. butter or margarine

1 tsp. sugar

1. Place all ingredients in a medium-sized saucepan, stir, and cover tightly. Cook over low heat for about 10 minutes or until carrots are tender and glazed (covered evenly with the thick liquid), and most of the remaining liquid has cooked away.

2. Stir to coat with remaining liquid and serve.

Preparation time: 20 minutes
Serves 4

Dessert Crepe Batter

4 eggs

1 c. all-purpose flour

2 tbsp. sugar

1 c. milk

¼ c. water

1 tbsp. melted butter

1. Beat eggs in a bowl.

2. Add a little bit of the flour and sugar. Use an electric mixer or whisk to combine. Then add a little bit of the milk and water. Mix. Repeat until all of the flour, sugar, milk, and water are added. Then beat with a whisk or electric mixer until smooth.

3. Beat in melted butter.

4. Chill batter at least 1 hour.

5. Cook in a crepe pan as described in the recipe for basic crepe batter on page 37.

Preparation time: 1 hour 15 minutes
Makes 20 to 25 crepes

Crepes with Strawberries/ *Crêpes aux Fraises*

These crepes can easily be filled with other kinds of fresh fruit. Try using 3 c. of blueberries or sliced peaches instead of the strawberries. Delicious!

3 c. fresh, sliced strawberries

⅓ c. granulated sugar

8 oz. (1 c.) cottage cheese

8 oz. (1 c.) sour cream

½ c. powdered sugar

10 to 12 dessert crepes
(see recipe on page 51)

1. Combine strawberries and granulated sugar. Set aside.

2. Beat cottage cheese in a blender or with an electric mixer until smooth. Add sour cream and powdered sugar and stir well.

3. Use about ⅔ of fruit and creamy mixture to fill crepes. Fold crepes over.

4. Top with remaining fruit and creamy mixture, or top with fruit and powdered sugar.

Preparation time: 30 minutes
Makes 10 to 12 crepes

Crepes with strawberries are pleasing to both the eye and the palate. For variety, crepes can instead be filled with blueberries, peaches, or other fruit.

Pears Helen / *Poires Hélène*

¼ c. chocolate syrup

4 to 8 scoops vanilla ice cream

4 canned pear halves, drained

⅓ c. raspberry or strawberry jam

1 tbsp. hot water

1. In the bottom of each of 4 sherbet glasses or bowls, put 2 tablespoons chocolate syrup.

2. On top of syrup, place 1 or 2 scoops of ice cream.

3. Place pear half, cut side down, on top of each portion of ice cream.

4. Combine jam and water in a separate bowl and spoon mixture over each pear.

Preparation time: 15 minutes
Serves 4

Pears Helen, or poires Hélène, is a flavorful medley of chocolate, pears, and jam that goes well with any meal.

Chocolate Mousse/Mousse au Chocolat

Chocolate mousse is often made with unsweetened chocolate and has a bitter, strong flavor. This recipe, however, is for a light, sweet-tasting mousse that is sure to appeal to all chocolate lovers.

1 envelope unsweetened gelatin powder

¼ c. cold water

2 squares unsweetened baking chocolate

1 square semisweet baking chocolate

½ c. milk

½ c. sugar

1 pt. heavy cream

1. In a medium bowl, combine gelatin with water and set aside.

2. In a medium saucepan, combine milk and chocolate. Over low heat, stir until the chocolate is completely melted. Add the sugar. Stir until it dissolves completely. Let cool.

3. In a medium bowl, use an electric mixer to beat the heavy cream until it thickens and forms soft peaks.

4. Pour the chocolate mixture into a large mixing bowl. Use a spoon to combine the gelatin mixture with the chocolate.

5. Use a rubber scraper to fold one-third of the cream into the chocolate. Fold in remaining cream.

6. Pour into an attractive serving bowl or into individual serving dishes and cover with plastic wrap.

7. Cool in the refrigerator for at least 2 hours or overnight. Decorate with whipped cream or grated sweet chocolate before serving.

Preparation time: 15 minutes,
Chilling time: 2 hours
Serves 4

Holiday and Festival Food

In France food itself is reason to celebrate. French chefs are known around the world for their exceptional culinary skills. Imagine, then, the care that goes into meals prepared for family and friends in honor of special holidays and festivals. Family members gather in the kitchen for hours to prepare the food, talk, and laugh.

The recipes that follow take advantage of the fresh fruits and vegetables available during the holidays for which they are prepared. The recipes are simple, but the results are scrumptious. As you sit down with friends to savor the foods you prepare, remember to enjoy the time as the French would. Bon *appétit*!

The Yule log is a traditional Christmas dessert in France. (See recipe on page 66.)

Traditional Leg of Lamb with White Beans/
Mouton aux Morgettes

I lb. dried white (Great Northern) beans

8 c. water

I tbsp. margarine or butter

4 small onions, finely chopped

I clove garlic, minced

2 small tomatoes, peeled* and seeded**

2 tbsp. thyme

2 c. water

I- to 3-lb. leg of lamb

4 to 6 cloves garlic

I tbsp. margarine or butter

salt to taste

I tbsp. fresh parsley, finely chopped

1. Place the beans in a large pot and cover them with 8 c. water.

2. Boil beans for 15 minutes. Drain and set aside.

3. In the same pot, melt the butter on low heat. Add the onions and sauté for 3 to 5 minutes, or until translucent.

4. Add the beans, the minced garlic clove, tomatoes, thyme, and 2 c. water.

5. Cover the pan and simmer on low heat for 1 hour and 30 minutes. Stir occasionally. If water evaporates, add another cup.

6. While beans are simmering, heat oven to 425°F. Wash meat under cool water. Pat dry with a paper towel. Place the leg of lamb in a roasting pan.

7. Peel 4 to 6 cloves of garlic and slice each of them down the middle. Make small cuts in the sides of the roast and insert garlic.

8. Sprinkle the meat with salt and bake for 30 to 45 minutes. (Allow 10 to 15 minutes of baking time for each pound.) Baste frequently with drippings.

9. Sprinkle finely chopped fresh parsley over the beans. Dot the beans with butter or margarine when ready to serve with the lamb.

Preparation time: 2 hours
Serves 6

*To peel a tomato, place it in a small saucepan of boiling water for about 1 minute. Remove with a slotted spoon and cool until the tomato is warm but no longer hot. Use a small paring knife to peel off the skin. It will come off easily.

**To seed a tomato, cut the peeled tomato in half and use a paring knife to cut out the seeds.

Fresh Asparagus with Aioli / *Asperges à l'Aioli*

Asparagus:

1 lb. asparagus

½ tsp. salt

4 tbsp. (½ stick) unsalted
    butter*

salt and freshly ground pepper
    to taste

Aioli:**

1½ c. reduced-fat mayonnaise

4 garlic cloves, peeled and pressed

1½ tbsp. lemon juice

1½ tbsp. Dijon mustard

¾ tsp. dried tarragon

1. Rinse the asparagus and cut off the woody ends.

2. Fill a steamer with about an inch of water. Add the asparagus to the basket. Cover and steam for 5 to 10 minutes, depending on the size of the stalks. Drain and pat dry with paper towels. Rinse with cold water to stop the cooking and then dry with paper towels.

3. **To make aioli:** While asparagus is steaming, combine mayonnaise, garlic cloves, lemon juice, Dijon mustard, and dried tarragon in a bowl. Refrigerate. (Makes 1½ c.)

4. Top the cold asparagus with aioli or classic vinaigrette (recipe on p. 36).

Preparation time: 15 to 20 minutes

*For a low-fat alternative, sprinkle hot asparagus with a little lemon juice instead of adding butter or margarine.

**Aioli may be stored in the refrigerator in a tightly sealed jar for up to one week.

Asparagus with aioli can be savored at holidays or anytime fresh asparagus is available.

Strawberry Tartlets / *Tartes aux Fraises*

Crust:*

1½ c. flour

pinch of salt

1 tsp. sugar

4 tbsp. butter, chilled and
    cut into pieces

1 egg slightly beaten

½ tsp. vanilla extract

Filling:

2 lb. fresh strawberries,
    stems removed

10 tsp. raspberry or strawberry
    preserves

whipped cream or nondairy topping

chocolate shavings (optional)

**If you do not have miniature tart tins,
look for mini tart crusts in the freezer
section at the local grocery store. Bake
as directed on the package.*

1. Preheat the oven to 325°F. In a large bowl, mix together the flour, salt, and sugar.

2. Add butter to the flour mixture. With a fork or pastry blender, work the butter into the dry ingredients until small "pebbles" begin to form.

3. Add the egg and vanilla. When the dough begins to stick together, use your hands to shape it into two large balls. Wrap the balls in plastic wrap and chill for 20 minutes.

4. Remove from the refrigerator. Roll dough out on a lightly floured surface with a rolling pin.

5. Place the miniature pie tins face-down on the dough. Using a paring knife, cut around the tins. Transfer the dough to the tins. Bake for 10 to 15 minutes or until the crust is golden and cooked through.

6. Just before serving, spread 1 tsp. fruit preserves on the bottom of each tartlet. Top with 4 or 5 fresh strawberries and a dollop of whipped cream. Sprinkle with chocolate shavings.

Preparation time: 15 minutes
Chilling time: 20 minutes
Baking time: 10 to 15 minutes
Serves 10

Yule Log/Bûche de Noël

Filling (Vanilla Pastry Cream):

2 tbsp. cornstarch

1 c. 1% lowfat milk

1 tsp. pure vanilla extract

1 large egg

1 large egg yolk

3 tbsp. sugar

1. Place the cornstarch in a small nonstick saucepan. Whisk in ¼ c. of the milk until smooth.

2. Whisk in the remaining ¾ c. milk.

3. Bring the mixture to a boil over medium heat, stirring constantly. Reduce the heat to low and cook for one minute. Remove from heat. Add the vanilla extract.

4. In a small bowl, beat together the egg, egg yolk, and sugar. Continue stirring while you stir in a small amount of the warm milk mixture (2 to 3 tbsp.) to the egg mixture. (This will keep the eggs from cooking when you add them to the saucepan.)

5. While stirring the milk mixture in the saucepan, add the egg mixture.

6. Cook the egg-milk mixture over low heat, stirring constantly, for 1 minute, or until the mixture has thickened.

7. Use the pastry cream warm or chilled. Store in a sealed container in the refrigerator for up to two days.

Cake:

4 large egg whites

½ c. granulated sugar

4 egg yolks

1½ c. plus 2 tbsp. sifted
all-purpose flour

1 tbsp. powdered sugar

*If you don't have a jelly-roll pan, you
can use a cookie sheet.*

1. Preheat the oven to 400°F. Line a jelly-roll pan* with parchment paper.

2. In a medium bowl, combine egg whites and 3 tbsp. of the granulated sugar. Beat with a mixer on medium speed until soft peaks form.

3. Beat in ¼ c. of the remaining granulated sugar. Beat on high speed until the whites are stiff and shiny.

4. In a large bowl, combine egg yolks and the remaining granulated sugar. Beat with the mixer on high speed until the mixture is pale and airy.

5. Using a rubber spatula, fold the egg whites into the yolks. When well blended, carefully fold in the flour until well mixed.

6. Spoon batter into the prepared pan and spread evenly. Bake 9 minutes, or until lightly browned. Remove from the oven and place the pan on a wire rack. Let stand for 5 minutes.

7. Dust a large piece of parchment paper with powdered sugar. Carefully turn the cake onto the paper. Spread the pastry cream over the surface of the cake. Using both hands, roll the cake lengthwise into a tight log.

8. Lift the parchment paper and transfer the cake to a serving platter; remove paper. Sprinkle yule log with powdered sugar.

Preparation time: 45 minutes
Serves 8

King's Cake / Galette des Rois

To serve the galette des rois, place the crown on top of it. Cut into slices. Whoever finds the bean will be crowned king or queen for the day.

1¼ lb. frozen puff pastry, thawed

2 eggs

7 oz. pure almond paste*
    (softened)

1 dried bean (such as a pinto,
    kidney, or Great Northern bean)

1 cardboard crown (available at a
    dime store or party store)

*If you cannot find pure almond paste in the grocery store, make the recipe for Vanilla Pastry Cream on page 66. Substitute almond extract for the vanilla extract.

1. Preheat the oven to 425°F. On a piece of wax paper, use a rolling pin to roll the puff pastry into a disk ⅛-inch thick. Use the wax paper to transfer the disk to a greased cookie sheet.

2. In a medium bowl, mix 1 egg with almond paste until smooth. Spread the mixture evenly onto the pastry. Place the bean on the almond paste.

3. On the wax paper, roll out a second disk ⅛-inch thick. Place this disk on top of the almond-filled disk and press it down tightly around the rim.

4. In a small bowl, use a whisk or a fork to lightly beat the remaining egg. Use a pastry brush to spread it on top of the disks.

5. Bake the galette for 20 minutes, then lower the temperature to 400°F.

6. Continue baking for another 25 minutes or until golden brown. Serve warm.

Preparation time: 15 minutes
Baking time: 45 minutes
Serves 8

Index

About the Author

Lynne Marie Waldee, a native of St. Charles, Minnesota, graduated from St. Olaf College in Northfield, Minnesota, with a degree in political science. Later she graduated from Vanderbilt University Law School in Tennessee. She went on to work as a municipal bond lawyer on Wall Street in New York City.

Waldee has loved to cook ever since the second grade, when her mother taught her how to make gingerbread cookies. She has traveled widely in France and has studied classical French cooking with instructor Peter Kump in New York City. In addition to French cooking, Waldee enjoys reading, traveling, and collecting antiques.

Photo Acknowledgments The photographs in this book are reproduced courtesy of: © Robert Fried, pp. 2–3, 10, 16; © Robert L. Wolfe, pp. 4 (left), 31, 44, 54; © Louiseann / Walter Pietrowicz, September 8th Photography, pp. 4 (right), 5 (both), 6, 28, 32, 35, 40, 47, 53, 57, 58, 63, 64, 69; © Charles & Josette Lenars/CORBIS, pp. 13, 14; © TRIP/H. Rogers, p. 24.

Cover photos: Front top and back, © Louiseann/Walter Pietrowicz, September 8th Photography; front bottom and spine, © Robert Fried.

The illustrations on pp. 7, 17, 25, 29, 30, 33, 34, 43, 45, 48, 59, 62, 65, 67, and 68 and the map on p. 9 are by Tim Seeley.